EY UP AND AWAY!

BY VICKY RYDER

D1799118

With thanks to
Stacy Makishi, Pat Crawford and my family,
who all love to laugh.

Ey Up and Away!

~

Growing Up in Nuneaton, a Town in the Wild West Midlands

BY VICKY RYDER

Ey Up and Away!
Growing Up in Nuneaton,
a Town in the Wild West Midlands

by Vicky Ryder

ISBN 978-0-957074-90-3

Published by Wandering Star Press
London, New York, Honolulu
www.wanderingstarpress.com

Cover and typesetting: gnibel.com

CONTENTS

STARDUST

"And now the purple dust of twilight time..." sang my father,
as we sifted coal through the garden sieve...
"... steals across the meadows of my heart".

It was a lovely, warm, spring day and my father and I were
half way up the coal tip, scratching around to pass the time.
He'd been made redundant and liked to keep himself busy.

"Now there's a song for you. Stardust, by the great Nat King
Cole. Your mother loves that song".

My father had a lovely, dark brown voice; like chocolate. He
would serenade my mother sometimes and she would swat
him away, smiling and tight lipped, all the while loving it.

His song smouldered on like the coals beneath us, and I
smouldered along with him, word perfect.

"Dad...where's Reverie?"
"How do you mean?"
"You know...like, lost in Reverie."
"Oh! That Reverie. It's in America. It's a massive place. Very
easy to get lost in. I was lost there myself once."

"What were you doing in America?", I asked.
"I was a stand in for Clark Gable".

"Did you ever meet Sophia Loren?", I sighed.

I was deeply in love with Sophia Loren. I had thought it was probably a lost cause until I caught a glimpse of her husband, Carlo Ponti, on television. He was an old, fat bloke and I had been very cheered by the sight of him.

'Yep, poor old Sophia Loren. She's got T.B. you know", said my father.
T.B.! I was stricken with horror.
"Ar. Two beauties!". My dad chuckled at his own joke.

"Tut", I raged.

I relaxed and thought of Sophia's eyes, her lips, her curves.
"So, did you meet her?", I asked.
"Meet her! I'd have married her if I hadn't been promised to your mother. Oh yes, she thought the world of me"

I thought Sophia Loren was the height of sophistication and I wished that I was Italian or at least that I could speak Italian.

"Dad, can you speak Italian?"
"Yes, of course I can", he said, smiling weakly.
"Will you teach me?"
"Yes, if you like."

Within a week I could count to ten. Uno, duo, rolo, polio, volcano, mussolini, semolina, impetigo, pisa, malteser.

My dad knew everything.

TEA TOWEL

"He said, "You're never old enough to have a twenty year old daughter", said my mother, pursing her lips and smiling in a gesture of false embarrassment.

"He just couldn't believe it".
She was referring to the new bus driver who had mistaken my sister, who had Down Syndrome, for a half fare.

"You want to watch him" said my Nan, tossing a newly shelled pea into her mouth.

And with that my mother snapped a tea towel out into the air and folded it into a near perfect square.

EGG AND LEMON

"Greasy or normal?" said the hairdresser.
"Is it medicated?" shouted my Nan towards the flabby back
 fiddling at the shampoo rack

"No, egg and lemon or beer".
"Only, I don't really like medicated, it reminds me of nits",
 said my Nan.

"It's not medicated, Beattie, it's egg & bloody lemon.
 Medicated is something else entirely", said the hairdresser,
 with a look of boiling indifference smeared onto her face.

"What do you think, then?" said my Nan.
"Shall I have the beer?"

"Well, if you do, your old man'll be able to find you in the
 dark!", said the hairdresser, her mules slapping the lino.
"Oooh, better make it egg & lemon then", said my Nan,
 silently convulsing.

FRIDAY IS FISH

"Where have you been?", she said to the driver, as she pulled me up the steps of the bus.

"Yes, all stood here waiting in this flipping wind!", said the woman behind us.
Fat legs and bottoms hit the seats and there was a mass expulsion of trapped air from beneath them.

"I've been stuck behind a fire engine in Heath End Rd", said the driver to no-one in particular.
"Next door to the Labour Club went up. Chip fat"
"Is it Friday then, Nan?" I asked.
"Be quiet and sit still" she said.

ENVY

Trevor Littler's willy is dancing in the beam of my flashlight
in the hot, musky depths of the cupboard under the stairs.
I can't decide if I want it
or if I want it, so instead,
I hit him.

WYATT EARP

My grandmother's neck went rigid.
"He's undone himself. Don't look", she said.

"He's been had up for this before and he used to be in the
Salvation Army".

I peered over at the man, aching for a good long look at his
private parts, in much the same way that I had ached to be
Wyatt Earp.

The man caught my eye and I returned his stare without
committing myself to any particular emotion.

He flipped his penis out and jiggled it up and down.

I stared as fast as I could.
These things didn't last long and you had to be quick.
Like a road accident or someone crying in a public place.
It would be over before curiosity could be satisfied.

THE NEW TIMEX WATCH

The shopping bags landed with a thump on the kitchen floor and she raced past me to the toilet.
"I've done a bit in my pants", she shouted, as I timed her wee with the red second hand of my new Timex watch. Fifty four seconds. Disgusting. I hoped it would never happen to me.

"Tea up, Mother" shouted my mother towards the back toilet, and my Nan emerged blowing her relief into the air like cigar smoke.

She looked down at me disapprovingly.
"Todger Moss showed himself off on the bus again and Madam here sat staring at him, as bold as you like".
"It was brilliant, Mother". "It was purple", I ventured. "You should have seen it".

My mother shook her head, looking at me as though there might have been a mix up at the hospital.
"Dirty beggar", said my Nan. "He wants locking up".

I yearned to be dangerous and to this end had forced the boys in my street to have a look at my own private parts, even to touch them. But they had not been frightened. Merely bored and obedient.

"You've got to feel sorry for the family though, haven't you? said Nan. "She's a lovely girl. She works in the hairdresser's on the corner of Pool Bank and Abbey Green. She works like a dog and there's him showing his damned tackle to all and sundry, the pig! It's awful."

"At least he's not off messing about with other women, like some", said my mother. "And he's very good to her. He's turned that house into a palace. They've even got a cocktail bar".

My grandmother thrilled to this new information and grabbed it like a hungry hyena.

"Cocktails!, she sneered, What do they want with cocktails? He wouldn't know a cocktail from Ash Wednesday!".
"How about a Bloody Mary?", I ventured.
"How about a bloody clip round the ear?", she said....and meant it. "I'd rather have a man who knows what's what than a damned cocktail bar".

I tried desperately to feel sorry for the man's family but could only see them surrounded in glory.
The glory of their tragedy.
They were like the Kennedy's.
They would salute and lose legs to cancer.
Their eyes would shine with a shared sadness and they would be beautiful.
All because of one small, purple piece of flesh that should have stayed nestled inside a pair of Co-op pants.

"Why didn't you tell the bus driver, Mother?" my mother asked.
"What, and have to change hairdressers?" said my Nan.
"Don't be daft".

NAN

You slid so easily towards death;
As though on a moving staircase in an airport.
Lighthearted and girlish, you laughed at the spirits dancing
in front of your eyes.
Eyes that had seen nothing for twenty years.

Your body had reduced itself to that of a child, when once
it had frightened me with its sturdiness. I had thought
the coffin empty in the Chapel of Rest and peered over
to discover your tiny frame, hiding, skin smooth, more
beautiful than ever you were in life.

"They're all waiting for me", you said, and I had no doubt
that you were right. I envied you this journey; going home
at the speed of light.

And when you finally skipped away, unwitnessed, there was
no self-recrimination on our part; no guilt.
You simply had no need of us who were left in the old world.

Like a kite that escapes its owner, there was a moment of
shock, grief for that which was lost, followed by joy as I
watched you soar,

So high
So high
So high

LUCILLE BALL'S QUIFF

"Hair has got to be trained", said my mother, as she pushed
the headband under my fringe and scooped everything back
off my face. My hair was as straight as the Coventry Canal
and it grew stoutly and relentlessly in one direction only.
Forward.

She had knocked up the headband herself with a piece of
green, Madras checked cotton and some spare elastic. The
elastic rubbed the sides of my head raw where the top of
my ears joined my face.

"It will only go back if trained over a number of months" she
said, frowning.

I imagined my mother in a spangled leotard with a chair in
one hand and a whip in the other, training my growing hair,
like an angry lion.

When the headband came off for bed, my hair ached
from root to tip until it settled itself back down again and
became a good old fringe.

After three weeks she admitted defeat. But this was only
round one. My mother was made of sterner stuff where the
matter of fashion was concerned.

"We'll curl it back with the tongs", she cried, in a flash

of inspiration one night, half way through 'Double Your Money' with Michael Miles. The tongs were similar to nutcrackers, only long and thin and she shoved them deep into the heart of the coal fire. Pulling them out again, she spat delicately on them, her lips barely parting, her tongue darting quickly in and out again.

Ladies spitting.

She combed a piece of my shining hair up into the air and clamped it between her fore and middle fingers.

In went the tongs and she rolled them swiftly down towards my head. I withdrew my neck like a tortoise. "Don't be such a baby", she snorted. "I shan't hurt you".

Moments later she was searching for the Germoline and I was left with one large curl at the front of my head and a stinging burn beneath.

To pass the time and take my mind off the pain, I tried to make my mouth look like Lucille Ball's. My father came home from work looking remarkably like Desi Arnez and said, "Something's burning". He sniffed his way over to me and said "Has she been buggering about with the electrics again?

"Don't be so daft" said my mother.
My father raised his eyebrows to me in a gesture of solidarity.

DEAD DOG

I can see my mother ahead of me, walking along the
riverbank, the cold evening wind pulling at her clothes.
She's just a little too far away for my puppy eyes to focus.
Too far upwind to catch her scent.

I run to catch up with her, to grab her smooth, stockinged
legs. This small town Ava Gardner who belongs to me.

As I reach her side, there is an almost imperceptible
movement. She pushes me with her elbow, ever so slightly,
and over I go. I surface head first like a newborn. Shock
forces my mouth wide open and I suck air hard and deep
into my body. I'm as cold as ice.

I'm down twice more before I remember I can swim.

My mother carries on walking, not even breaking her stride.
But then she turns, ever so slightly, and smiles.
"You can swim", she shouts over her shoulder, as a passing
stranger drags me out like a dead dog, onto the bank.

Years later, I question her about this.
"You always had to be right on top of me", she says, not
understanding that if she had only asked, I'd have jumped.

Whenever you want a cigarette—
remember...

Player's please

PLAYER'S NAVY CUT CIGARETTES · MEDIUM OR MILD

JUNIOR SERVICE

"Eddie! Don't you dare give that child a cigarette", shouted
my mother, through the back kitchen window.

My father and I were crouching behind the shed, he
explaining to me that if Sir Alec Douglas blinking Huuume
wanted to be called Huuume, he shouldn't have spelled it
Home, and that we should never compromise on this issue.

With that, he offered me a puff of his Senior Service.
I accepted and blew out a stream of smoke that
unfortunately shot around the corner of the shed and gave
the game away.

"Eddie! Don't give her cigarettes", said my mother.
"Never mind, our babby!", said my dad.
"We'll swap to a pipe".

RAMBO

"Rag and Bone", "Rag and Bone".

His voice hit the still, Sunday afternoon air like a tidal wave
hitting a cliff, and had approximately the same impact on
my six year old ears.

The rag and bone man came to our street with his horse
and cart every two or three months and he was laden with
indescribable treasures, the like of which we only saw at
Christmas and birthdays. Bubbles, chalk, pencils, pop guns
and whistles.

You could buy his goods with old clothes, worn out prams
and almost anything that could be found in the back garden
of any council house in Nuneaton.

"Oh, bloody hell, here we go", said my dad, as I looked at
my mother with an expression of overwhelming, desperate
need.
"Mum, will you find me something?", I begged, rushing to
the window to check if any of the other kids were yet out
of their front doors.
I caught sight of Pam and Barry Orton dragging two lead
pipes and a toilet over the grass as fast as they could go.

Panic rose within me. "Mother! Hurry......it'll all be gone!"

My mother, who had shot up the stairs like Roger Bannister and descended them like Sir Edmund Hilary in dire need of a cup of cocoa, appeared breathless in the living room with an armful of my dad's old pants and vests and an old pair of overalls.

"Ar!" said my dad, "I knew it'd be all my stuff went".

I shot out of the front door and joined the jostling crowd of kids who had gathered at the back of the cart, eyes wide with excitement and fear.
The fear of being too late.
By the time I got to the front there was nothing to be seen. Not even a balsa wood glider. The man saw the hope leave my eyes, to be replaced with studied indifference. I was embarrassed by my own need.

He took the clothes and tossed them towards the horse's rear end. I held my breath as he dragged a cardboard box towards him. He opened the lid and I heard tiny peeping noises. Inside the box were a frightened little crowd of baby chicks, no more than a couple of days old. He lifted one out and gave it to me and I cradled it's little, yellow body in my hands.

I carried it at a half run to the back garden and sat with my back against the wall. Placing it on the dirt, I offered it a piece of night scented stock. It stood stock still, beak wide open, crying, or so it seemed to me.

I suddenly had a brain wave.
I dragged the old tin bath over to the outside tap and filled it with water. I dropped the chick in and it sprang to life. It

went round and round the bath, its wings flapping furiously. I watched in a happy daze. I tossed in a few stock leaves to give the bath more of a pondy appearance, and went inside for tea.

When I returned later, the little creature lay dead; floating sideways, it's single eye staring milkily up to Heaven.

Later that night, I lay in my dad's arms, crying softly,
exhausted with grief, lips swollen and hot.
"Come on, now", he whispered into my hair.
"Anybody could mistake a chick for a duck".

"Look at the feet next time".

T R E A S U R E

I am gathering the jewels that are dropping from my
father's shoes. Tiny, gleaming shards of metal from the
factory floor; trodden on in the night shift.

He brings these treasures home and scatters them
unknowingly in his path.

He is a comet of piercing brightness and I am his wake.

TOMMY THE TENDERFOOT No. 8   TOMMY'S STALKING
"Keep up your end when you're stalking your foes."
(It might read in two ways as Tommy now knows.)

WILY WAYS

"Dad, do all capitalists eat their babies?"
"Ar, mostly, Tiny", said my dad.

I had recently spotted a dead giveaway for those people
who probably indulged in this type of act; their mouths.

Alec Douglas Home and Malcolm Muggeridge were
two fine examples. I had seen them on television and
their mouths stretched too far sideways, rendering them
incapable of speaking properly. They had obviously eaten
something peculiar.

And then, of course, there was the Royal Family. My dad
seemed to quite like the Royal Family. He'd shaken the
King's hand once when they'd visited Coventry. Perhaps
they weren't capitalists?

I decided to investigate the matter a bit further. We had a
big dictionary at school from which we learned a word a
day. I asked Mrs. Amos to get it down for me.

"What did you want to look up, dear?" she asked.
"Capitalist", I said in a half whisper.
"Goodness!" she said, in a tone of voice that instantly warned
me I was on dodgy ground. "And where have you heard
that?"

"On the wireless", I lied.

"Capitalist", she shouted rather shrilly, poking a fingernail at the page. "A person who invests money in business".

Well, that was my Nan in trouble. She'd been selling tea towels and pegs to the neighbours. My granddad got them from a man he knew.

As far as I knew though, she didn't eat babies, had a normal mouth and could speak properly, even though she was from Birmingham.

The following Sunday we were all sitting down for tea when I decided to broach the matter. "Nan, have you ever eaten a baby?"

My Nan had just placed a large spoonful of pink blancmange into her mouth.
She forced herself to swallow it.

Turning to my father, she said, "There's something very unnatural about this child. For one thing, her eating's peculiar. Gorgonzola, at her age? And for another thing, she's no interest in her appearance. Dead babies, indeed! A visit to the clinic wouldn't come amiss, I'm sure".

My dad seemed riveted by the food on his plate.

My mother looked bewildered. One thing I knew was that my Nan had neither confirmed nor denied the charge. Wily, those capitalists.

TWO BY TWO

"And Noah bore three sons".

The preacher's voice was as dark and oppressive as the oak panelling on every surface of the chapel. It settled on us like a November fog.

"Ham, Spam and Japheth."

That couldn't be right, it was probably Jeffrey, I thought to myself as I tore a bit of cuticle off my thumb. I was at Sunday School. The Wesleyan Reform Church in Heath End Road. Neither my mother nor my father knew what Wesleyan Reform was, but they did know free childcare when they saw it. It was a rare and precious thing and they opened their hearts unto the Lord and gave thanks.

"And God said unto Noah, go forth and make thee an Ark. And two of every living thing shalt thou bring into the Ark. And every creeping thing that creepeth upon the earth."

I stared into the roof. More oak. If ever I had seen a creeping thing, this preacher was it.

My friend nudged me in the ribs. Dawn the Prawn could do miraculous and horrible things with chewing gum. As I raised my gaze to her face, I caught sight of a pink gum bubble slowly pulsating in and out of her nostril.

Her face was expressionless apart from a small, mean gleam in her eye that said, 'I will make you laugh'.

The preacher droned on. "And I will cause it to rain for forty days and forty nights."

I had asked my father when all this rain had happened and he had told me it was during the Coventry holidays, every year. I had heard of the Ark before. We had sung, "Ark the 'erald Angels Sing" in Mrs. Amos' class last Christmas.

The Prawn nudged again. Two bubbles this time, one in each nostril. She looked like a little pink toad.

"And Noah was six hundred years old when the flood of waters was upon the earth."
"Ar, and I'm a Chinaman", said Mrs. Harcourt, who was given to unchecked outbursts now and again, due to the fact that she had fits and hated her husband, who had become over friendly with the district nurse. All heads went down and a little titter ran round the chapel.

Mr. Harcourt's face turned bright red and he jutted his chin up sharply to release a fold of hot fat from beneath his shirt collar. The brylcreemed tufts of hair on the back of his neck settled down again in neat rows that reminded me of a hedgehog's spikes coming to rest.

The chapel prickled with tension.

"All in whose NOSTRILS was the breath of life, DIED", shouted the preacher, glaring horribly in our direction.

I turned to the Prawn, who had turned to stone. She had stuck her eyelids up with two small pieces of chewing gum and the shouting had startled her. She had breathed in too hard and both nostrils were blocked solid. She sneezed. The chewing gum shot out of her nostrils and clipped the back of Mr. Harcourt's head rather smartly, causing him to swat at himself, fearing he was under a wasp attack or some such thing.

Mrs. Harcourt seized her opportunity and laid into the back of his head with gusto. Someone shouted, "Give him a good walloping, me duck!" Mr. Harcourt upped and made a dash for the door with the Holy Bible clamped onto the top of his head.

The preacher quivered. His thin lips stretched tight over his ratty little teeth. "Is it any wonder that God sends the waters to punish the sinful?" he asked.

There was a silence and then a little voice from somewhere near the back whispered, "No-ah". The congregation exploded with mirth.

WATERSPORTS

"Get up the front with the little 'uns, you gormless bugger", said Lardy Matthews landing his hard pump on the waddling behind of his younger brother, Tiny.

We were making our way through the streets to the canal. My mother had elevated me to near royal status. She had bought me a sixteen foot long, PVC covered canoe for £9 19s 8d from the local paper, and now nine of us were carrying it on our heads towards probable death.

There were no heads visible. Just eighteen legs marching roughly in unison.

The skinny ribs of the canoe bent dangerously to accommodate the various heights of the assembled line up. "Can we put it down a minute?, shouted Colin Morris. It's banging up and down on me head". He was too short for his place in the middle and each step we took seemed to be driving him further into the ground.

We could smell the canal getting closer. A heady mixture of wet vegetation and dead animals curled into our nostrils. We reached the railings by the towpath. Half of us shinned over the top, dropping like fat pieces of summer rain onto the dirt below.

Paul Lloyd got his trouser belt hooked up and dangled in mid-air.

"He looks like a piece of pork hanging in the butchers", said his brother Jacky.

"Ar, and you'll look like a piece of bloody pork when I get down", said Paul, glaring at him.

In an unprecedented act of charity, we got him down and passed the canoe over the top.

I stepped in first, being the owner and therefore the leader. Lardy Matthews came next. His popularity sprang from an untiring willingness to exhibit his genitalia at a moment's notice.

Finally we were all in. We draped the little kids on the front and back decks of the canoe and off we paddled. Our legs made a vee shape around each other's bottoms, like a giant fishbone. Lardy broke wind, to the general amusement of all and the boat began to rock from side to side. Screaming broke out as we skewed sideways across the canal towards a giant clump of brambles on the far bank.

The nose of the canoe and the unfortunate two on the front deck disappeared under the bush. There was a dreadful humming noise and the bush exploded with angry wasps. We frantically paddled backwards, the oars smacking into the arms and heads of those in front of us. Those on the front and back decks had fallen into the water and were trying to make their way to the bank when a dead dog floated by, which bought on a fresh bout of screaming and laughter. The canoe thumped into the bank and we dragged ourselves onto the towpath.

On March 16th, 1961 a ship went down off the coast of Nuneaton.

The casualty list was as follows:

The Captain — Two blisters

Lardy Matthews — One bleeding ear, one pair of Marks and Spencers underpants

Jacky Lloyd — Three wasp stings and a laceration to the back of the head

Pat the Bat Lloyd — Blackberry staining to skin and garments

Paul the Ball Lloyd — One clump of hair

Tiny Matthews — One large splinter

Diane Liversedge — One missing tooth, one pair of shorts

Colin Morris — One pack of five Woodbines, one box of England's Glory

Raymond Greenway — One very severe thumping from surviving crew, due to the fact that he was the one who finally put his foot through the bottom of the ship and sent her down.

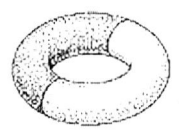

FIG. 2

WHAT GOES UP DOESN'T NECESSARILY COME DOWN

In my twelfth year, I decided to change sex. I decided to try being a girl.

My mother was very encouraging and took me into town for 'an outfit'. I came home with a camel checked mini skirt (four inches above the knee), slung low on the hips, with a wide belt: a blue, skinny ribbed, sleeveless sweater, and clumpy, brown shoes with a gilt buckle. My hair was feather cut, 'a la Julie Driscoll' and as was the fashion, I painted false lash lines under my eyes and covered my lips with Miner's white lipstick.

The general effect was that of 'spiders consume dead child'.

The reason for this transformation was that Vincent Barraclough had stopped me in the street on my way back from fishing and asked me out to the Youth Club.

As I sat on my tackle box toying with a maggot, I realised how like Elvis he looked, and as I couldn't be Elvis, even though I had the monogrammed Elvis in Memphis guitar, he was the next best thing.

We arranged to meet on Saturday night at the Donnethorne Inn. This was a favourite haunt of the local kids who would climb over the back fence, steal the empty pop bottles and take them back into the jug and bottle door to exchange them for threepence each.

Vincent had a pocket full of threepenny bits. We wandered up to the Youth Club. At some point, he took my hand in his and I noticed a wart on his knuckle, but it didn't matter. He had beautiful, brown eyes with long, black lashes and white, white teeth. As we walked into the Youth Club I felt a surge of smug pride. I liked this feeling.

I had moved smoothly from fishing to big fish, albeit in a tiny pond.
"Do you want a game of table tennis?, said my heart throb.

I was rather good at table tennis, due to the fact that my Mum had bought me a set for Christmas and we often played on a gigantic piece of hardboard which we had dragged onto an old table in the shed. "Yes, ok", I said, picking up a bat.

We knocked the ball back and forth for several minutes, getting into a rhythm, while 'Na, Na, Hey, Hey, Kiss Him Goodbye' blared in the background. We sang along, happy and pleased with ourselves.

A little crowd had gathered to watch us play. Suddenly I missed a return. The ball bounced off the table, hit the floor between my feet, shot up between my legs and didn't come down. Everyone held their breath and waited. I shook my leg. Nothing. I was mystified. Someone started to laugh and within seconds, the laughter spread around the room as I stood and debated whether to peer up my skirt. I put the bat down and walked to the door with my cheeks aflame. I ran all the way home. My mother hovered over me with a look of touching concern and later when I undressed for bed, we found the ball.

There was a three inch gap in the hemming stitch of the skirt and the ball had lodged itself inside the hem.

Vincent, to his credit, asked me out again. This time I took him fishing.

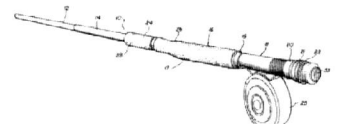